CLOUDS

BILL McAULIFFE

SCIENCE OF THE SKIES

Published by Creative Education
P.O. Box 227, Mankato, Minnesota 56002
Creative Education is an imprint of The Creative Company
www.thecreativecompany.us

Design and production by Liddy Walseth
Art direction by Rita Marshall
Printed by Corporate Graphics in the United States of America

Photographs by Corbis (Atlantide Phototravel, Bettmann, Paul Edmondson, Warren
Faidley, Momatuik/Eastcott, Jim Reed/Jim Reed Photography, Visuals Unlimited),
Dreamstime (Greg Blomberg, David Davis, Peter Sjokvist), Getty Images (Central Press/
Hulton Archive, Kazuko Kimizuka, Fred Ramage/Keystone, Paul Souders, Allan
Tannenbaum/Time & Life Pictures, The National Gallery of Scotland, Travel Ink, Vincent
Van Gogh, Whitworth Art Gallery), iStockphoto (Don Bayley, Glenn Culbertson, Paige
Falk, Luca Di Filippo, Uwe Lol, Florea Marius Catalin, Andrei Nekrassov, Patrick Oberem,
Dave Raboin, Styve Reineck, Yali Shi, Mark Stahl, Maurice Van Der Velden, Ingmar
Wesemann, Philippe Widling, Peter Zelei)

Library of Congress Cataloging-in-Publication Data
McAuliffe, Bill.
Clouds / by Bill McAuliffe.
p. cm. — (Science of the skies)
Summary: An exploration of clouds, including how these masses of water vapor
develop, the different forms they can take, and how extreme examples of clouds have
impacted human history.
Includes bibliographical references and index.
ISBN 978-1-58341-926-7
1. Clouds—Juvenile literature. I. Title.

QC921.35.M43 2010
551.57'6—dc22 2009023505

CPSIA: 120109 PO1095

First Edition
2 4 6 8 9 7 5 3 1

CREATIVE ⬤ EDUCATION

CLOUDS

BILL McAULIFFE

SCIENCE OF THE SKIES

WHEN THERE'S NOTHING ELSE TO DO ON A FINE SUMMER DAY, CLOUDS MAKE GREAT ENTERTAINMENT. "NOTHING IN NATURE RIVALS THEIR VARIETY AND DRAMA," WRITES GAVIN PRETOR-PINNEY, AUTHOR OF *THE CLOUDSPOTTER'S GUIDE.* INDEED, COTTONY PUFFS GLIDING DREAMILY ACROSS A BLUE SKY CAN GRAB THE IMAGINATION AND SUDDENLY POPULATE THE HEAVENS WITH DOGS AND DRAGONS, BIRDS AND BATTLESHIPS, TRUMPETS AND SNEAKERS, OR A MAP OF FRANCE. BUT THE SURPRISES DON'T STOP THERE. THOSE PUFFY CLOUDS MIGHT SWELL INTO THICK MASSES HIGHER THAN THE TALLEST MOUNTAINS AND THROW OUT LIGHTNING, THUNDER, HAIL, RAIN, OR EVEN TORNADOES. THEN THEY'LL MOVE ON, GIVING WAY TO THE HARMLESS LITTLE CARTOON CLUMPS THAT MESMERIZED US EARLIER. AS SIMPLE WISPS OF ICE OR WATER VAPOR MILES ABOVE US, CLOUDS CAN SIGNAL WHAT WEATHER IS COMING. BUT AS COMPLEX MACHINES MAKING LIFE-SUSTAINING RAIN OR DEVASTATING STORMS, CLOUDS ARE ALSO THE FACE OF WEATHER ITSELF: SOMETIMES WELCOME, SOMETIMES THREATENING, ENDLESSLY FASCINATING.

THE CLOUD FACTORY

We always look up to see clouds. But the process of making clouds begins all around us, including sometimes right at our feet. When the sun hits the earth, it warms up the surface. Warm air always rises, because it's lighter than cold air. This fact alone explains much of how the world's weather works. But clouds help us see it in action.

When warm air begins rising from any surface on Earth—the ground, lakes, rivers, or the ocean—it sucks moisture up with it. This process causes water to **evaporate**, and as the word suggests, it involves vapor—in this case, water vapor. On a humid day, it's easy to sense that there's more water vapor in the air than usual. But water vapor is always invisible.

The air above us is usually cooler than air on the ground, which is absorbing the sun's rays and warming up. Generally, the higher the altitude, the cooler the air, which is why some mountains have snow on their peaks even in summer. As water vapor continues to rise, the cooler air around it causes it to **condense**, or change into visible water droplets. And when enough water droplets form and swirl together, hundreds of trillions per cubic foot of space, they make a cloud that can hide the sun or swallow an airplane.

That's only the beginning, of course. If the day has heated up enough and there's enough moisture available, the small, white cloud of water droplets, light and buoyant on the rising warm air, might swell and join with others. As more vapor flows up into the growing cloud, it cools, and more water droplets form. This cooling releases heat, which has to go somewhere. The heat moves upward, forcing the cloud to billow even farther into the sky.

Then the process gets complicated—and even dangerous. In the cloud's core, massive amounts of warm air can rise upward at 25 to 70 miles (40–113 km) per hour. Often, the cloud swells high into the atmosphere—10 miles (16 km) or more—where it reaches very cold air. If it gets so high that it can't rise any farther into the cold air of the atmosphere, or if it runs into strong high-altitude winds, the cloud can spread out into an **anvil** shape that is characteristic of a serious storm cloud.

High, cold air is usually an essential ingredient in the process that forms clouds, such as these cirrocumulus clouds floating over a tropical mountain range.

In such a towering cloud, the water droplets can actually get colder than the temperature at which they'd normally freeze. Water in this state is called **supercooled**. When supercooled droplets latch on to some tiny solid in the air—dust, smoke particles, or grains of sand, for example—they freeze instantly. If they get heavy enough, they fall to the earth as hail, which can damage rooftops, rip leaves off trees, ruin crops, and even break windshields. And as anyone who's ever been caught outside in a hailstorm has probably learned, hail can hurt people, too.

As hail tumbles through the cloud, it might melt and fall to the earth as rain. In any case, rain and hail carry cooler air with them as they fall, so now the cloud has both warm updrafts and cool downdrafts. And the gentle white clump that passed over our yard earlier in the day may have joined with others in forming a menacing mass of clashing energy. Out of that clash may come not only rain and hail but the two features that have filled humans with fear and awe for thousands of years: thunder and lightning.

Nearly every civilization throughout recorded history has put its most powerful gods in control of thunder and lightning. This is not surprising. But as famed American statesman and inventor Benjamin Franklin proved in 1752 when he flew a kite into a lightning

The formation and disappearance of clouds is a cyclically vertical process—water vapor rises skyward initially, and it later often returns to Earth as rain or hail.

Despite their soft and fluffy appearances, clouds can possess powerful and potentially deadly energy, as they reveal in the form of lightning during thunderstorms.

KILLER CLOUDS

Tornadoes are some of the most concentrated destructive forces in nature. But that's only when they're on the ground. Indeed, a rotating funnel cloud, even if it has a tail, isn't defined as a tornado until it touches down. Tornadoes can have winds that blow from 65 to more than 200 miles (105–322 km) per hour. While a tornado, like any cloud, is made visible by condensed water vapor, tornadoes also appear to have a dark shroud at ground level. That shroud is the whirling dust and debris the tornado has picked up in its travels across the landscape.

storm, there are practical explanations for these awesome phenomena.

As raindrops, hailstones, and ice crystals fly up and down inside a cloud, negatively charged **electrons** get stripped off the rising elements and collect on the falling ones. The result is a positive electrical charge at the top of the cloud and a negative charge at the bottom. Positive charges also gather on the ground in a sort of shadow that follows the cloud. These opposites attract, as they do in a magnet, and if the charges get strong enough, they create a pathway for electricity—a lightning bolt, either between the cloud and the ground or within the cloud. Most lightning occurs within clouds, because the charge that builds there is stronger than the charge that builds between the cloud and the earth.

A bolt of lightning generates a temperature of about 54,000 °F (30,000 °C)—five times hotter than the

A cloud-to-ground lightning strike often actually involves several bolts of electricity along the same path, but it happens so quickly that it appears as a single bolt.

surface of the sun. That extreme and sudden heat warms the air around it, causing the air to expand rapidly. Thunder is the sound of that expansion. And because sound travels much more slowly than light, we always hear thunder after we see the lightning that causes it.

Clouds can form in other ways, too. Warm air moving toward a mountain might be forced upward and cool in the higher altitude, causing water vapor to condense into water droplets. This will make a cloud form above the mountain.

There are also man-made clouds. Power plants, which often emit warm air from tall stacks, send plumes into the sky which can become clouds or even fog. Jet planes form long white streaks of condensation called contrails when the warm exhaust from their engines spills into the cool air at high altitudes. People can even make clouds themselves by breathing outside on a cold day. The small puffs that leave our mouths or nostrils are made visible by the same process that creates the clouds high above us. Warm air (breath) meets cold air, and water vapor condenses into tiny but visible water droplets, producing our small, personal clouds.

Contrails (above) occur regardless of season, as they are generally formed thousands of feet up; power plant plumes (opposite) are most visible in cold weather.

Clockwise, from above: Claude Monet's The Cliff at Dieppe, *Vincent Van Gogh's* Wheatfields under Thunderclouds, The Fortifications of Paris with Houses, *and* Wheat Field with Cypresses.

THE ART OF CLOUDS

Clouds turn up frequently in art, sometimes for their beauty, but more often for their darkness or ability to conceal things. French musicians and painters of the 19th and early 20th centuries seemed to have a special sense of cloud wonder. Composer Claude Debussy and Parisian jazz guitarist Django Reinhardt both wrote famous pieces entitled "Nuages," which is French for "clouds." Many 19th-century French **Impressionist** painters such as Vincent Van Gogh and Claude Monet captured the moods and drama of clouds. Indeed, because they focused more on light and color than on objects, the Impressionists' works show a particular delight in clouds.

THE HIGH CLOUDS

There are days when the sky above may be so flaw-lessly blue that gray clouds and rain might seem impossible, like a bad memory. But that rarely lasts long. A short while later, thin, wispy clouds might appear overhead or come from the horizon, fine as horses' tails or the strokes of a paintbrush. These are *cirrus* clouds, the highest of the familiar clouds and often the first to appear—literally out of the blue.

Cirrus clouds travel at about 16,000 to 45,000 feet (4,900–13,700 m) above the ground on fast-moving air currents that can push them at 100 miles (160 km) per hour. Because they're so high, in very cold air, they're made up entirely of ice crystals, which is why they appear so delicate. Amid the high winds, they typically get stretched out into long, feathery shapes. And if cirrus clouds sometimes look like banners, that's fitting, because they often come with a mes-sage: the weather, so beautiful when they appear, may be about to change. They usually herald the beginning of a march of clouds across the sky, in weather systems that move from west to east across most of North America. The high clouds are often fol-lowed by lower and thicker clouds, which frequently bring rain or snow before clearing, making way for blue sky again and completing a never-ending cycle.

Cirrocumulus clouds drift at about the same altitude as cirrus clouds but are instead a mat-like collection of small, puffy clouds. Cirrocumulus clouds are more substantial than cirrus clouds because they contain supercooled water droplets in addition to ice crystals, but they aren't dense enough to cast shadows. Each clump of a cirrocumulus cloud is sometimes regarded as a cloudlet, or a small cloud of its own. When these cloudlets arrange themselves in long rows or bars that stretch across the sky, they create a formation that has long been described as a mackerel sky, because it resembles the scales of the mackerel fish. When the water droplets in a cirrocumulus cloud freeze, they sometimes make a form of precipitation called virga, which is ice or snow that can fall from the cloud in vis-ible tails or thin curtains but which evaporates before it reaches the ground.

Relatively little water vapor rises high enough to become part of cirrus clouds, a cloud type that occurs with regularity over North America regardless of the season.

Cirrostratus clouds have almost magical properties. Essentially vast sheets of ice crystals floating at 16,500 to 30,000 feet (5,000–9,100 m) above the ground, cirrostratus clouds are not sharply defined during the day. But they're what makes a blue sky sometimes look white. They might also cast a halo around the sun, or, especially in winter, generate bright dots on either side of the sun in spectacular phenomena known as sundogs or parhelia. Depending on how the sunlight reacts to the ice crystals, the sundogs might be white or broken into colors like a rainbow. The halo phenomenon is even more pronounced at night, when a cirrostratus cloud can cast a bright ring around the moon. The presence of a cirrostratus cloud often means that precipitation can be expected within 12 to 24 hours.

A halo around the sun is created in much the same way as a rainbow: rays of light from the sun are refracted, or bent — by ice crystals in a halo, water droplets in a rainbow.

CLOUD NINE

It was once common to describe a person who was blissfully happy—or knocked unconscious—as being "on cloud nine." This usage may go back to the International Cloud Atlas, first published in 1896. That publication listed the 10 major groups of clouds so that cumulonimbus clouds appeared 9th on the list. It's easy to imagine how being on top of a cloud perhaps 10 miles (16 km) above the ground would make a person a little giddy. The International Cloud Atlas is still published by the World Meteorological Organization and has specific names for nearly 60 types of clouds in the 10 major groups.

The altostratus-created "red sky at night" has been a reliable weather sign for thousands of years; even the Bible contains references to this colorful phenomenon.

Altostratus clouds also stretch thinly across the whole sky, at elevations between 6,500 and 23,000 feet (2,000–7,000 m). Made of water droplets and ice, they are gray or blue-gray in color and thicker than cirro-stratus clouds, and while the sun can shine through them, they filter enough rays that they eliminate shad-ows. Somewhat featureless and apparently unmoving, altostratus clouds are generally regarded by **meteo-rologists** as the most boring of clouds. Nevertheless, these are the clouds that account for the age-old weather saying, "Red sky at night, sailors' delight; red sky at morning, sailors take warning." That's because when a rising or setting sun peeks from an area of clear sky under a layer of altostratus clouds, the low angle of light will cause the clouds to glow red, often in spectacular displays. If it happens at sunrise, it often means the cloud blanket is approaching the sun from the west and that foul weather may be coming. If it happens at sunset, it often means a daylong cloud cover is breaking open from the west toward the east, with clear skies to follow.

Puffy clouds often tightly packed at 6,500 to 18,000 feet (2,000–5,500 m) are known as *altocumulus* clouds. These clouds, being lower in the atmosphere, where temperatures are above freezing, are made almost entirely of water droplets. This makes them denser than most of the other high- and mid-level

While altocumulus clouds (pictured) can sometimes resemble the streaming "mares' tails" formed by cirrus clouds, they hold significantly more water vapor.

clouds, and they don't allow light to pass through, which gives them the appearance of having dark bottoms and light tops. Altocumulus clouds on summer mornings often are followed later in the day by thunderstorms, because they frequently form ahead of **cold fronts**. Like cirrocumulus clouds, altocumulus are large fields of cloudlets that appear in almost orderly ranks. But they are lower and larger than cirrocumulus. From the ground, altocumulus cloudlets appear about as big as the width of one to three of a person's fingers held at arm's length.

One of the most dramatic cloud formations is a high-altitude type of altocumulus known as a **lenticular** cloud. Sometimes stretched out into a lens or almond shape, lenticular clouds occasionally startle skygazers or photographers into thinking they have seen a flying saucer. Other versions have enough height that their smooth, silky surface resembles a spinning top. Lenticular clouds are most common in mountainous areas, because they are formed by air rushing up and over mountains. Just as water flowing over a rock will form a hump or "standing wave," warm air flowing over a mountain that cools and then condenses in the higher air will form the same sort of shape. Indeed, this type of air flow has helped **sailplane** pilots set world records for both distance and altitude. Lenticular clouds travel at 20,000 feet (6,100 m) and higher.

Even higher than the cirrus clouds—much higher, in fact—is a unique formation known as a **noctilucent** cloud. Most common at far northern or southern latitudes near midsummer, these clouds travel at about 30 to 50 miles (48–80 km) up, near the cold borders of outer space. They are visible only at night, when they catch the rays of the sun long after it has set. Scientists think the clouds might be made of water vapor that has condensed on dust particles that drift down from the upper reaches of the atmosphere.

Two of the more mysterious clouds are the noctilucent (top), whose name means "night shining," and lenticular (bottom), which resembles science fiction spacecraft.

LATIN IN THE LABEL

There are nearly 100 cloud varieties. Each carries at least one of five Latin-based terms describing its key characteristics. It's the same system of genus and species distinction that's used for plants and animals. Knowing the genus names and how their Latin meaning translates to meteorology is the best way to begin identifying clouds.

Alto: *High or deep*
Cirrus: *Hair or fringe*
Cumulus: *Heap or mass*
Nimbus: *Storm or shower*
Stratus: *Stretched or spread*

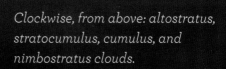

Clockwise, from above: altostratus, stratocumulus, cumulus, and nimbostratus clouds.

THE LOW CLOUDS

If there's one cloud type that is the classic cloud, it is the *cumulus.* These are the clumpy clouds that every child draws, as well as the clouds depicted on the seal of the American Meteorological Society. These gentle forms scattered randomly across the sky float only 2,000 to 3,000 feet (600–900 m) above us. They are warm-weather clouds because they are formed by small thermals, or water vapor riding on quickly rising air that's been heated by the sun. So low to the ground, they are made entirely of water droplets and appear white on the top and dark on the bottom. And although they are the image of lightness, in reality an ordinary cumulus cloud might weigh several hundred tons because of its massive water content.

Cumulus clouds are not very high above us, and they travel on winds that might push them as fast as 25 to 40 miles (40–64 km) per hour. But if there's enough rising warm air and water vapor available, they can swell into great masses, sometimes expanding upward as high as 45,000 feet (13,700 m). There they meet a ceiling of cold air in the atmosphere that stops them from rising any farther, and their tops often spread into a wide anvil shape that is characteristic of a severe storm cloud. In the tropics, where warm air and water vapor are always plentiful and the atmosphere is higher, cumulus clouds might reach 60,000 feet (18,200 m). That's more than twice as high as Mount Everest, the world's tallest mountain peak. When cumulus clouds mass at high altitudes, they are known as *cumulonimbus* clouds, the most fearsome type of storm cloud, capable of dropping hail and heavy rain and generating lightning and thunder. It could be said that the cumulus cloud starts out as a low cloud with high ambitions.

With their dark and often ground-hugging forms, low clouds—such as these drooping mammatus clouds—frequently have a more ominous appearance than high clouds.

The brooding cousin of the cumulonimbus is the *nimbostratus* cloud, a low, broad, gray mass that is heavy with moisture and often brings long-lasting rain or snow. Nimbostratus are the deepest, or thickest, of the broad, layering clouds, extending from bases at about 2,000 feet (610 m) to tops at about 18,000 feet (5,500 m). Their bottoms often appear ragged as they drop rain or snow, but they are invariably thick and

Among the very lowest of the low clouds is mist, which commonly occurs during the cool hours of the morning and then "burns off" as the sun rises in the sky.

dark enough to hide the sun and moon completely. Nimbostratus clouds are almost always associated with a weather front, the border between warm and cold air masses.

The *stratus* cloud is a vast, gray, dull sheet of cloud that can blot out the sun for days. Stratus clouds envelop everything from the ground up to 6,500 feet (2,000 m). A stratus cloud can bring drizzly weather but rarely heavy rain. Unlike cumulus clouds, which form on small, local updrafts, stratus clouds are the result of large areas of warm and cool air meeting, as when a weather front passes through.

Stratocumulus clouds, as the name suggests, have features that are common to both stratus and cumulus. Typical after a siege of rain, stratocumulus are both clumpy and sheet-like, covering the sky but letting shafts of sunlight through or offering glimpses of blue sky. Stratocumulus clouds swirl about 2,000 to 6,500 feet (600–2,000 m) up and are exactly what meteorologists mean by "mostly cloudy." They often show a wide range of grays and whites, making the sky look as if it were a black-and-white photograph.

One of the easiest clouds to identify and name is the *mammatus* cloud. Resembling the cows' udders or other animals' mammary glands for which they're named, mammatus are warm-weather clouds that hang in heavy sacs from the bottoms of many different types of clouds. They often indicate that heavy **turbulence** and storms are nearby; in fact, they frequently mark the bottoms of cumulonimbus clouds. Mammatus are formed in the opposite way from cumulonimbus—by a sinking rather than a rising motion. Cold air sinks out of the higher reaches of a cloud and condenses into water vapor in the warmer air below.

Two types of clouds that we can actually feel are *mist* and *fog*. These are in fact clouds—masses of extremely fine water droplets—that rest on the ground or water.

Nimbostratus clouds usually indicate that a rainy day is in store, as these moisture-laden clouds bring prolonged periods of light to moderate precipitation.

WARMING STREAKS?

All clouds reflect some of the sun's radiation from above and trap some of the earth's heat below. Some researchers believe man-made contrails may be adding to that effect and accelerating global—or at least regional—warming. The strongest effects are believed to be at night, when contrails, being an addition to Earth's natural cloud cover, aren't reflecting any radiation out but continue to seal some in. Warm nights may be a key signature of global warming. Some researchers believe the effects of contrails on climate will increase as jet travel increases, and that shifting flights to daylight hours might ease the problem.

The United States' National Oceanic and Atmospheric Administration defines them by how much they limit visibility. If a person can see more than five-eighths of a mile (1 km) but not farther than seven miles (11 km), the gray stuff is mist. If the visibility is less than five-eighths of a mile, it's fog, and a danger to drivers, pilots, and ships at sea.

Over land, fog is usually formed when cool air moves over warm ground. This can happen after a cooling rain. In autumn, when warm ground is evaporating moisture during cool nights, a type of fog called radiation fog is common. And in the spring, when warm air moves over remaining snow or ice, **advection** fog forms. Fog is also common in mountain and river valleys, where cool air can sink into low spots, causing moisture to cool and condense into a cloud, or fog.

In coastal areas, warm, moist air drifting over cool water generates extensive and often thick fogs. Off the coast of Newfoundland, warm air traveling north over the Gulf Stream often meets the cool water of the south-flowing Labrador current, enshrouding the Grand Banks region in fog up to 200 days a year. On the other side of the North American continent, a peninsula known as Point Reyes, just north of San Francisco, California, is similarly vulnerable to fogs. These are the continent's foggiest places.

FACES IN THE CLOUDS

Clouds don't last very long—sometimes they're around for hours and other times for mere minutes. But they've carried the same names for more than 200 years. In 1802, an amateur English meteorologist and chemist named Luke Howard proposed that clouds, while always changing, shifted through several definite stages or forms. He gave them the Latin-based names they have today. Howard, who also studied and wrote about the climate of London for 40 years, is widely regarded as the "Father of Meteorology." He recognized clouds as visible evidence of forces in the atmosphere and wrote that they were as revealing as a person's face.

London, England, which lies close to the North Sea, has been famous for its fogs for centuries. But it's also where the term **smog** was coined to describe the sometimes poisonous combination of smoke and fog. Because so many Londoners used to burn coal in their fireplaces, the air in the city was often filled with tiny particles of coal soot, something water vapor can cling to when it condenses into water. This made London's fogs often thicker than they might normally be, as well as a health hazard. In December 1952, a 4-day fog in the city was believed responsible for the premature deaths of 4,000 people due to respiratory problems. The disaster led to several clean air laws that restricted the burning of coal, and today there is little difference in the frequency of fog between London and the surrounding English countryside.

During the Great London Smog of 1952, about one million coal-burning stoves in the city produced filthy fogs so thick that Londoners called them "pea soupers."

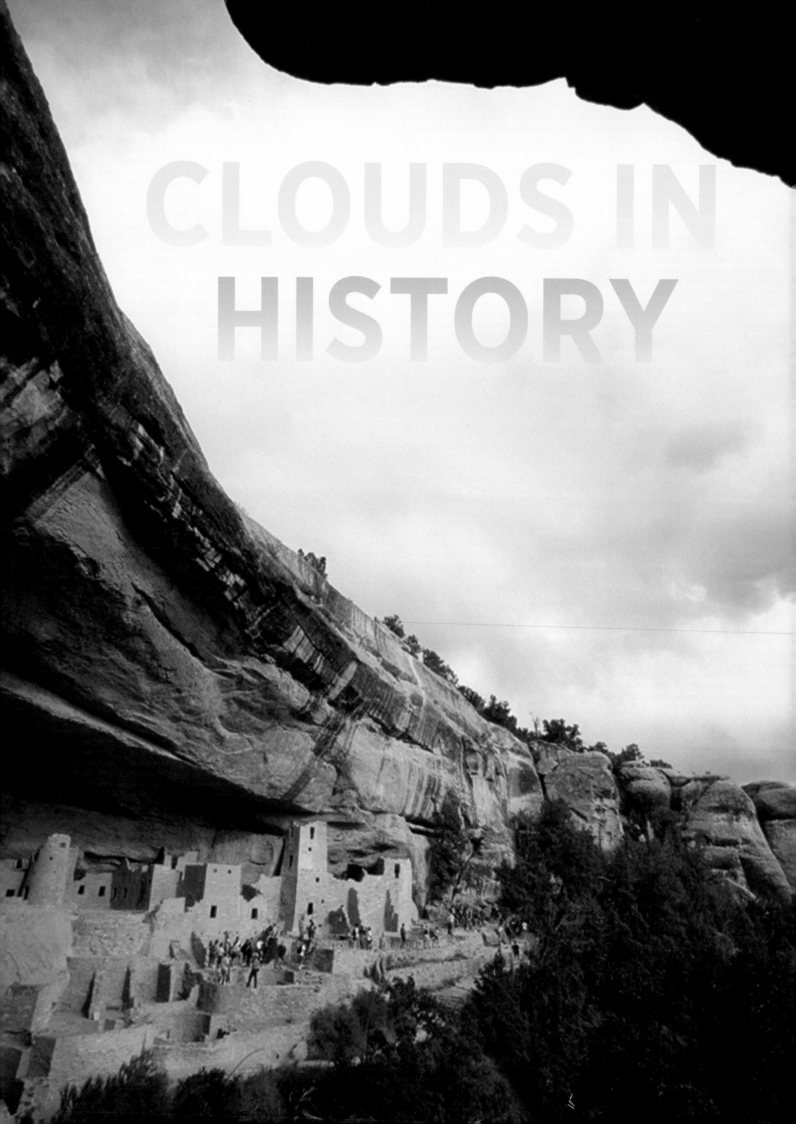

CLOUDS IN
HISTORY

In September 1777, things weren't going well for George Washington's Continental Army. It had just been defeated by the British at the Battle of the Brandywine and was retreating to protect Philadelphia, Pennsylvania, the capital of the new American nation. But when the British, under General William Howe, advanced after him, Washington decided to turn and face another battle, even with his troops outnumbered almost two to one.

But just as the two forces faced off in a valley about 20 miles (32 km) west of Philadelphia, a tremendous thunderstorm broke loose. One British commander noted that within minutes, the troops were mired in mud up to their calves. Even though no one fired a shot—their gunpowder was soaked and useless—the encounter became known as "The Battle of the Clouds" and an important moment in the Revolutionary War. Washington's vulnerable forces were able to retreat and regroup. Ultimately, they were able to turn the tide against the British and win America's independence.

History has shown time and again that the strongest military forces and political figures are often humbled—or sometimes favored—by the clouds and what they can bring. In 217 B.C., the armies of the famed **Carthaginian** general Hannibal hid in a hilltop fog near Lake Trasimene, about 125 miles (200 km) north of Rome, Italy, before descending on a Roman army. The surprise attack resulted in one of the Roman Empire's worst military defeats.

Similarly, some of the most dramatic conflicts of World War II were set on northern Europe's cloudy and sometimes cold stage. In 1944, the Allied invasion of Europe at Normandy, on the French coast along the often-stormy English Channel, required precise weather forecasting. Low clouds would prevent aircraft, including gliders, from dropping paratroopers behind the enemy defenses (a critical part of the Allied assault) the night before the beach landing. The mission was originally scheduled for June 4, 1944. But U.S. general Dwight D. Eisenhower postponed the invasion when his chief forecaster predicted stormy weather. Meanwhile, the German occupiers appeared to relax, not knowing that clearer weather was coming. Launched on June 6, the invasion was a success and opened the way for the Allies to reclaim France and western Europe from Nazi Germany.

Clouds can forever change cultures; the prolonged absence of clouds and rain in the late 13th century may have compelled the Anasazi people to abandon their ancestral homes.

In December of that year, the Germans tried to break apart the Allies' eastward advance. They believed winter's low clouds would keep the Allied planes grounded. In what became known as the Battle of the Bulge, German ground forces advanced in thick fog and made a deep dent in the Allied lines in Belgium. But in two days, the weather cleared, and the Allied air forces were able to begin a counterattack. Eventually, the Allies beat back the German advance, speeding the end of the war.

For thousands of years, entire societies have been built around the rhythms of clouds and rain. The ancient Egyptians, who lived in a desert climate, took advantage of seasonal rains and flooding along the Nile River and built one of the world's richest cultures on its banks.

Clouds can also discourage or end civilizations. In what is now the southwestern U.S., a sophisticated Indian tribe known as the Anasazi abandoned their elaborate

Weather played a huge role in 20th-century warfare, as combatants such as these American paratroopers were alternately cursed and assisted by the presence of clouds.

MAKE YOUR OWN CLOUD

To witness cloud formation up close, try this experiment. You'll need:

A glass or plastic jar with a wide mouth
Hot water
A match
Ice cubes in a plastic bag

Fill the jar with hot water. Let it sit for a minute. Pour out all but about an inch of the hot water. Light the match, hold it for a few seconds over the jar, then drop it in. Immediately cover the mouth of the jar with the ice cubes. The rising warm air will cool in the sinking cold air and condense on the smoke particles, forming a small cloud.

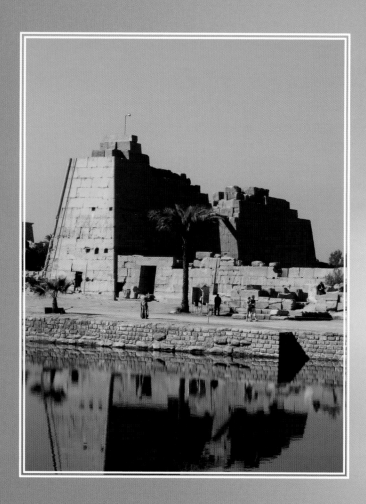

adobe villages in about A.D. 1300, after living there for centuries. Many archaeologists believe the disappearance of clouds and rain, part of a long-term change in climate, drove the Anasazi out because they could no longer grow enough food.

A similar tragic reversal of fortune happened on the Great Plains of the U.S. in the 20th century. Pioneer farmers, who had been led by promoters to believe there would be enough rain to grow crops, plowed up millions of acres of prairie, only to see the soil dry up and blow away when the rains stopped in the 1930s. That blowing soil created a type of cloud more menacing than any rain clouds, as tons of topsoil, lifted by strong winds, formed masses of fine dust that rolled across the landscape. Often these "clouds" were so dark that cities turned on their streetlights during the day. Cars on the highways stalled when dust choked their engines, and sailors on ships on the Atlantic Ocean sometimes found themselves wiping dust from the plains off their decks. Many people died of a respiratory ailment called "dust pneumonia" from breathing the darkened air.

Humans have tried to turn the tables by making clouds do their bidding. Prompted by peaceful intentions, people began experimenting with the process known as **cloud seeding** more than 60 years ago. They wanted to bring rain to dry areas, to reduce hail, and even to alter the course of hurricanes. Cloud seeding generally involves delivering particles of **silver iodide**, usually from planes or via rockets launched from the ground, into a moisture-filled cumulus cloud. The particles act as the **nuclei** on which droplets of super-cooled water can instantly freeze, causing them either to begin to fall to the ground—turning to rain, ideally— or to form hailstones so numerous that big, damaging ones can't form. The practice has brought, at best, mixed results to agricultural regions seeking moisture for crops. But considering the impact that weather can have on war, cloud seeding has also been viewed by some as a weapon. The U.S. military seeded clouds for six years during the Vietnam War, in the 1960s and '70s, trying to make the Ho Chi Minh Trail, a key supply route for the North Vietnamese, impassable with mud. It was never determined that the effort made a significant difference in the local weather.

Shortly after that war, more than 40 nations, including the U.S. and the then Soviet Union, signed an agreement intended to prevent nations from using **weather modification** as a tool in warfare. Even so, a U.S. Air Force study in 1996 asserted that the U.S. could "own the weather" by 2025 through technology. Key effects would be the ability to dictate battlefield conditions, including flooding the enemy,

The Battle of the Bulge featured some of the bloodiest—and coldest— fighting of World War II; under overcast skies, more than 150,000 men were wounded or killed.

THEY ONLY LOOK COMFORTABLE

While on a routine flight in 1959, U.S. Marine Corps pilot Lieutenant Colonel William Rankin ejected from his disabled jet 47,000 feet (14,300 m) over Virginia. Parachuting into a cumulonimbus cloud, Rankin endured temperatures of about –60 °F (–52 °C) and low air pressure that caused bleeding from his eyes. He was pelted by hail, yanked upward 6,000 feet (1,820 m) at a time by warm air, nearly struck by lightning, and deafened by thunder. He inhaled mouthfuls of rainwater. What should have been a 10-minute fall lasted 40 minutes. Although badly bruised, frostbitten, and in shock, he made a full recovery.

The absence of clouds and the
life-giving rains they carry can result
in great human misery, as illustrated
by the United States' "Dust Bowl"
of the 1930s.

or causing drought or lightning. The report also emphasized that the U.S. could accomplish something Hannibal may not have even dreamed of: making fog to conceal its own forces and removing fog from over the enemy.

So far, though, no one owns the clouds. And it's more likely that we owe the clouds a debt. With their infinite possible shapes and power, the clouds can often inspire us. But most critically, while bringing us the gift of water, they also sustain all life on Earth.

Although they can be dangerous when they give shape to storms, clouds—the face of Earth's weather— are more frequently welcomed and are almost always captivating.

GLOSSARY

ADOBE, n., adj. — *a bricklike building material made of clay and straw; also, a structure made from this material*

ADVECTION, n. — *the horizontal movement of air or water*

ANVIL, n. — *an iron or steel tool against which to hammer and shape metal; it is wide and flat on top of a smaller base*

CARTHAGINIAN, adj. — *of or from the ancient city of Carthage, on the North African coast of the Mediterranean Sea*

CLOUD SEEDING, n. — *the process of dispensing a substance into clouds in an attempt to make rain or reduce the size of hail*

COLD FRONTS, n. — *the foremost edge of moving masses of cold air*

CONDENSE, v. — *to form a liquid from a vapor*

ELECTRONS, n. — *negatively charged particles within atoms; atoms are basic units of nature that cannot be broken down into smaller units*

EVAPORATE, v. — *to turn from a liquid into a vapor*

FROSTBITTEN, adj. — *suffering frostbite, which is damage to skin tissue from freezing*

IMPRESSIONIST, adj. — *describing an artistic style created in 19th-century France that emphasized atmosphere, light, color, and mood*

LENTICULAR, adj. — *describing a type of cloud shaped like a lens or almond that often appears on the downwind side of a mountain*

METEOROLOGISTS, n. — *scientists who study weather patterns, weather phenomena, and other behaviors of the atmosphere*

NOCTILUCENT, adj. — *lit at night*

NUCLEI, n. — *cores or centers around which things are grouped; the plural form of "nucleus"*

RADIATION, n. — *in weather terms, the giving off of heat*

SAILPLANE, n. — *an airplane without an engine that flies on updrafts of warm air after being towed aloft by another plane*

SILVER IODIDE, n. — *a powder used as an ingredient in rainmaking; its crystalline structure is similar to that of ice and encourages water vapor in clouds to freeze to it*

SMOG, n. — *fog or haze that has a high level of pollutants such as smoke or dust; the word is a combination of "smoke" and "fog"*

SUPERCOOLED, adj. — *describing a liquid that is below normal freezing temperatures but remains in a liquid state*

TURBULENCE, n. — *violent motion or instability*

WEATHER MODIFICATION, n. — *an effort to change weather patterns and outcomes through artificial means*

Egan, Timothy. *The Worst Hard Time: The Untold Story of Those Who Survived the Great American Dust Bowl*. Boston: Houghton Mifflin, 2006.

Farndon, John. *Extreme Weather*. London: Dorling Kindersley, 2007.

Kids Science News Network. "How Do Clouds Form?" National Aeronautic and Space Administration. http://ksnn.larc.nasa.gov/k2/s_cloudsForm.html.

Legault, Marie-Anne, ed. *Scholastic Atlas of Weather*. New York: Scholastic, 2004.

Lynch, John. *The Weather*. Buffalo, N.Y.: Firefly Books, 2002.

Pretor-Pinney, Gavin. *The Cloudspotter's Guide*. New York: Perigee, 2006.

University Corporation for Atmospheric Research. "Clouds in Art." http://www.windows.ucar.edu/tour/link=/art_and_music/cloud_art/cloud_art_main.html.

USA Today. "Understanding Clouds and Fog." http://www.usatoday.com/weather/wcloud0.htm.

INDEX